McCall Collection of Modern Art

Ernst, Miró, and the Surrealists

by ENRICO CRISPOLTI

Published by Fratelli Fabbri Editori,
Publishers, Milan, Italy, and

The McCall Publishing Company
New York, New York

Illustrations Copyright © 1970, in Italy,
by Fratelli Fabbri Editori, Milan, Italy

PUBLISHED IN ITALY UNDER THE TITLE *Mensile D'Arte*
ALL RIGHTS RESERVED. PRINTED IN ITALY
Library of Congress Catalog Card Number 76-106656
SBN 8415-1010-5

Surrealism, Breton, and Painting

Surrealist art came into being at the end of World War I to answer the cry for a new and "more nearly honest" way of seeing, of thinking, of being. It was not merely a new artistic movement self-consciously created to contrast with the avant-garde movements that had gone before—Expressionism, Cubism, Futurism, Dadaism—it was, rather, a truly basic change in the way people wrote and painted and, consequently, read and saw.

That Surrealism was far more than a passing fad is attested to by the attraction it has for young men and women today. This most self-searching and self-aware of generations lights up at Miró, Dali, Magritte, De Chirico, Max Ernst. The cry for a "more nearly honest" world is everywhere today and Surrealism still fits, or perhaps fits particularly well, the taste of our time.

"The positive values [the Surrealist painters] advocated—*the reinterpretation of the human personality and the rescuing of man from the abyss into which he has fallen*—outweigh the [movement's] shortcomings and inconsistencies" (P. Waldberg). Thus its legacy is as appreciated today as when Breton wrote his famous first *Manifesto.*

André Breton was Surrealism's greatest spokesman, a polarizer of those artists and writers, wherever they might be, who responded to the cry for a new vision. His has been a leading historical role not only in heralding the new but in making use of many of the earlier insights and creative examples that ran from French and German Romanticism through Symbolism to the avant-garde movements of the first two decades of this century. It was he who gave Surrealism a precise, doctrinal form closely linked to the psychoanalytic discoveries of Freud.

The Great Breakthrough: De Chirico

Giorgio de Chirico is unquestionably the inventor of super-reality or Surrealism in painting. As early as 1910, De Chirico, who was then twenty-two, began to create a largely people-less world in which the urban environment was caught in a series of scenes and architectural elements having all the characteristics of the Italian cities in which he was then living: the empty piazza, the colonnade with its seemingly fixed shadows, the house wall, ochre or red perhaps, with its single window, single plant on the window ledge, the single statue, holdover of a now clearly anachronistic ancient world, impersonal and motionless, the stretched perspective, anti-Renaissance in feeling with its limitless, lonely vision — what Joseph-Émile Muller calls "the intensity of emptiness of those squares" — the apparent suspension of life. It is as if all the world were taking a siesta and the ambiance people have created for themselves stands alone, *unguarded,* posing the frightening question: Why all this? What does the scene mean? Is this truly all?

Nearly all the major Surrealist painters were influenced by De Chirico's painting and, in the artist's world of extreme, perpetual identity crisis, it is quite surprising to find that almost none of them found it hard to admit, even to proclaim, the startling impact that their early confrontations with this painting had on them.

By the time De Chirico's vision had caught the rapt attention of other painters, he had largely concluded his Piazzas and Porticoes stage and had passed on to Specters, then to Mannequins — the entrance on stage of the human form but depersonalized, poised in a featureless attitude that summed up a man's or woman's situation at a given moment in time as if there were no tomorrow. Beautiful in their arrested movement, the figures in these paintings are like the childern's game of living statues — only for the mannequins there can be no resumed movement.

By 1924, when Breton's famous first *Manifesto* appeared, De Chirico was looking for new styles; the metaphysical painting he had pioneered ("a worrying relationship [exists] between perspective and metaphysics," he had written) no longer satisfied him. As so often happens, his departure from the ranks he had led soon caused bitterness and flailing resentment. He went his way, having contributed in that initial period masterpieces that challenged the accepted vision and opened new vistas to modern expression in painting.

Breton mentioned De Chirico in the *Manifesto* of 1924, but he considered Francis Picabia, Marcel Duchamp, and Picasso typical Surrealist painters; Miró, Klee, Man Ray, Max Ernst, and André Masson rounded out Breton's horizon of phenomenology as exponents of creative Surrealism, which he himself fully exemplified on the literary plane.

"I believe," Breton wrote, "in the future resolution of those two states which at first blush seem so contradictory — dream and reality — in a sort of absolute reality, a super-reality, if one may so express it." And he created a definition, much as might a lexicographer, giving his peremptory, definitive understanding of the word "SURREALISM, *n.*: Psychic automation in its pure state, by which one progresses to express — orally, by means of the written word, or in any other manner — the actual functioning of thought. Dictated by thought, in the absence of any control exercised by reason, exempt from any aesthetic or moral concern. *Philosophy*: Surrealism is based on the belief in the superior reality of certain forms of previously neglected associations, in the omnipotence of dream, in the disinterested play of thought. It tends to ruin once and for all all other psychic mechanisms and to substitute itself for them in solving all the principal problems of life."

Characteristics of Surrealist Imagery

Beyond this basic statement, the *Manifesto* of 1924 offered precise guidelines for the formulation of a way to read and understand Surrealist imagery. Breton returned to a definition given in 1918 by Pierre Reverdy, a poet of latter-day Cubism, in a manifesto that appeared in *Nord-Sud*. Reverdy headed this magazine in Paris in 1917-18, and, together with Pierre-Albert Birot's *Sic,* it was an important mouthpiece for Cubists, Dadaists, and proto-Surrealists. "The image is a pure creation of the spirit," Breton wrote, citing Reverdy. "It cannot be born of any comparison, but only of bringing together two more or less distant realities. The more the interconnections between the juxtaposed realities are both distant and 'correct,' the stronger the image will be — and the greater its emotional power and poetic reality."

What Breton categorically denied was that an original image can be premeditated. Analyzing a poetic image such as Reverdy's "The day unfolded like a white tablecloth," Breton says, "It is false, in my view, to claim that 'the spirit has caught the relationships' of two realities so placed as to confront each other. To begin with, nothing has been captured at the conscious level. When we bring two opposite poles together in whatever fortuitous way, a special light is sparked — the light of the image to which we are infinitely sensitive. The value of the image depends on the beauty of the spark; it is, therefore, the function of the difference in potential between two conductors. When this difference scarcely exists, as in this simile, no spark is produced. Accordingly, we must concede that the two terminal poles of the image are not deduced one from the other by the intellect as it calculates the spark that is to be produced; rather, they are the simultaneous products of an activity we call Surrealist. Reason, on the other hand, is confined to recognizing and evaluating the luminous phenomenon."

As to the "shared qualities" of Surrealist images, Breton stated: "For me the strongest image is the one that presents the maximum degree of arbitrariness: the one that requires the most time to be translated into practical language; the one that encompasses an enormous charge of apparent contradiction, whether because one of the poles has been mysteriously withdrawn, because it promises to be sensational only to fade away, because it finds in itself ridiculous 'formal' justification, because it comes from the realm of hallucination, because it lends the mask of the concrete to the abstract (or vice versa), because it implies the negation of some elementary physical property, or because it releases laughter."

The Surrealist image is, then, not to be interpreted as the key to some symbolic form of communication, much less does it have an allegorical function. It is to be understood in terms of its own essential arbitrariness and of the emotive and evocative potential that such arbitrariness creates. Naturally, this potential operates within the widest margin of ambiguity and semantic multivalence so as to involve the onlooker actively in a "happening."

On the other hand, an amplified interpretation of the prescription for the "secrets of Surrealist magic art" is contained in the Breton *Manifesto* of 1924. It relates to automatic writing: "Put yourself in the most passive, or receptive, state possible. Abstract yourself from your own mind, from your own talents, and from those of others....Write rapidly, without a pre-established subject, and so hurriedly that you do not pause and are not tempted to re-read....Trust in the inexhaustible nature of the murmur."

Clearly, many of the formulations concerning Surrealism were more easily applied to poetry and prose than to the plastic arts.

The Wide Range of Surrealist Techniques

Surrealist painting approached the gradual solution of its problems along two main lines: one was figurative, that is it was based on the process of automatic formulation and association of images; the second was strictly nonfigurative, based on direct automatic writing. The first could well be exemplified by the works of Salvador Dali, René Magritte, Yves Tanguy, Max Ernst (and, obviously, the early De Chirico). And the second by the works of Duchamp, Picabia, Arp, Miró, Ernst, Masson, and Matta. Naturally, trying to establish a precise distinction between the two lines of development would be arbitrary and artificial. The Surrealist artist was free in the selection of his figurative means, and often (as was typical in the cases of Ernst and Masson) he could pass from figurative to nonfigurative in a single work.

The painters constituting the group came from various backgrounds, but they had already in their earlier experiences shared tendencies toward fantasy in their art. Joan Miró (b. 1893 near Barcelona) had submitted to many influences before his adherence to Surrealism: Fauvism in his youth in Spain, Cubism in 1919 after his acquaintance with Picasso in Paris, and Dada by the time of the last great Dada exhibition in 1922. Nevertheless, his natural innocence and simplicity made him thoroughly and for his entire career a true Surrealist, causing Breton to say that Miró was "possibly the most Surrealist of us all." (Chipp, *Theories of Modern Art*, p. 372.)

By the mid-twenties the aware public could hail the existence of important Surrealist sculpture—the works of Giacometti, Alexander Calder, and Max Ernst. There was also an extremely large production of Surrealist objects; the range of collateral techniques that may be made in one way or another to fit

4

into the graphic field is wide but minor in its revelatory power when compared to that of the paintings themselves.

The phenomenological and historical perimeters of Surrealism are not always limited to the happenings within the Breton group. Although André Breton was unquestionably the central force enunciating the theories of Surrealism, and his famous volume *Surrealism and Painting* (published in Paris in 1928 and published with successive amplifications in New York in 1946 and again in Paris in 1965) is still the authorized treatise of the movement, not all of Surrealism is confined to the Breton group. Furthermore, that group itself has over the years been subject to changes brought about both by inner dissent on the so-called poetic plane and by outer pressures due to historical phenomena.

The Dadaist Inheritance

Breton's experience before the *Manifesto* of 1924 had been gained in that cultural melting pot, the Paris Dadaist group, toward the end of the second decade of the century and the beginning of the twenties.

Tzara, the leader of the Zurich Dadaists, who was, with Hugo Ball, the prime mover of the Cabaret Voltaire in 1916, and the spirit behind the review *Dada*, which started publication in the middle of 1917, was in Paris at the beginning of 1920. The young Parisian creative talents had been working through the *Manifesto Dada, 1918*, which was published in Zurich at the end of that year. The *Manifesto* had made a lively impression in the French capital, profoundly influencing Aragon, Breton, and Soupault, who were about to launch their review, *Littérature*. In the last three issues of *Littérature* for 1919, Breton and Soupault published the first chapters of a text they both signed, "Magnetic Fields," and which Breton himself, in his 1924 *Manifesto*, defined as the "first purely Surrealist work," an example of automatic writing. Yet by this latter definition it was preceded by lyric texts of Picabia written in 1917, and by passages from *The First Celestial Adventure of Mr. Antipyrine* by Tzara, published in 1916. Breton was, of course, firmly reminded by others of these earlier publications.

In *Manifesto Dada, 1918*, Tzara had written: "I destroy the file drawers of the mind as well as those of organized society: everywhere demoralization, our hands moving from heaven to hell, our eyes from hell to heaven, and back on the road with that great seminal wheel of the universal circus in all its fantasy and in the real possibilities it releases in each individual....Once and for all, we need strong, straight, precise, un-understood works. Logic is a complication. Logic is always false...."

Breton and other Surrealists went along with Tzara's intent to "demoralize," with his battle against the falseness of logic, his anti-literary precepts, but they did not intend to limit themselves to gestures alone, dear as these were to Tzara. They were unwilling to limit themselves to the merely destructive. They wished to launch a movement, to indicate the possibilities of radical renewal, to promote a positive plan. The freeing of the true function of thought from rational control, brought about by automatism, thus opened the horizon for exploration and imaginative research—a far different outlook from the pure abstract and nonlogical line of Dadaist work as Tzara conceived it.

Tzara's 1918 *Manifesto* stated that "any pictorial or plastic work is useless; let it at least be a monster capable of terrifying the lackey-spirited, and not the honeyed food-bar decorations dear to those animals dressed up as men; let them not be illustrations of the squalid fable of humanity. A painting is the art of having two lines, which geometry proves parallel, meet on a canvas before our eyes, according to the reality of a world based on other conditions and possibilities. This world is neither specific nor definite in the work; it belongs in all its innumerable variations to the spectator. As far as its creator goes, this world has no causes nor is it based on theories. *Order=disorder; i=non-I; affirmation=negation:* the supreme splendor of an absolute art—absolute in the purity of a cosmic and ordered chaos, eternal in the life of a bubble without breath, without light, without control."

Arp's abstract works and the strongly ironic mechanical creations of Picabia and Man Ray, then Duchamp's everyday objects "designed" by the artist with little or no changes (the "ready-mades"), or the collages of Max Ernst are the most extreme radical examples, culminating in "anti-art," the negative landscapes of Tzara.

Nonetheless, Zurich's Dadaism initially accepted the rallying cry of *Futurism* and the work of De Chirico. André Breton, in his *Manifesto* of 1924, mentions Duchamp and Picabia as typically Surrealist, and recalls the subsequent experiments of Man Ray, Max Ernst, De Chirico, and André Masson. That is to say that, running parallel to the tradition of the abstract image or of the Dadaist pure object, there is the visionary tradition pioneered especially by De Chirico but also by Max Ernst, a tradition that originated in central and north European Romanticism, passing through the English Pre-Raphaelites to Symbolism.

The Symbolist Inheritance

Breton wrote, in a brief article on Symbolism: "We opposed a radically different world to the painting we considered no more than a leisurely dissertation on the second-rate—we sought a re-creation of the world in terms of the interior needs of the artist. Now sensation no longer takes first place but the most profound desires of the heart and spirit. The virtually senseless spectacle that nature and man's actions offer the common viewer ceases to be an aim and, instead, becomes an obstacle. An unsuppressable desire takes over which does not let go until it has torn the subject apart in order to extract those elements the artist needs from it, those that he can use with originality in relation to himself. This type of painting is obviously the only one that fulfills Rimbaud's desire for a language that speaks 'of the soul for the soul,' while all we can ex-

6

pect from the other type of art might be an attack of goose-flesh. The one is in relation to the other what poetry, in the best sense, is to prose of the best-seller and journalistic type. It is well known that this concept of art—the same as was held by the Primitives—went rapidly downhill from the Renaissance on, but the majority take every precaution against recognizing the enormous efforts made during the nineteenth century to save the integrity of this concept."

This historical interpretation, identifying the remote origins of Surrealist painting, does not exclude another element that we might call a-historical. This element implies figurative manifestations that differ in motivation among themselves but which agree fundamentally in their final results: they are based on the "absence of any control exercised by reason."

The remote origins of Surrealist painting—those which certainly cannot be considered obvious forerunners but can nonetheless be quite accurately defined a posteriori as discoveries—go back as far as Paolo Uccello's *Battle of San Romano,* the work of Piero di Cosimo, Arcimboldi, and Baldung, and they take on greater body and consistency during the Romantic period from such precursors as William Blake to the visionary quality that is one of the fundamental aspects of Goya's work, the morbid, nightmarish strain of Füssli, and the symbolic unreality of Casper David Friedrich. In fact, here we enter into the very cultural matrix from which were dredged the notions and words of Surrealism and Supernaturalism (Novalis, Heine, Gérard de Nerval, Victor Hugo): the new movement was conceived not as an evasion of or a breaking away from reality but as a greater penetration into it, departing from the basic plane of naturalistic rationalism. In *Surrealism and Painting* Breton said: "Everything I love, everything I think and feel, leads me to a particular philosophy of immanence according to which Surrealism is contained in realism itself, being neither superior nor inferior to it."

Böcklin and Klinger, with at least some coincidental contributions from Kubin, supplied the basic influence for the young De Chirico in Munich—in addition to the works of Schopenhauer, Weininger, and Nietzsche, of course. Böcklin's paintings were, for several years, works from which De Chirico actually copied, and they were especially valid for him because of their nostalgia for classical myths, which De Chirico turned into alarming presences full of psychological meaning and insinuations of unease, until he reached the full expression of his Metaphysical painting in 1910.

It was Klinger, the etcher, who suggested to De Chirico that rarified atmosphere and metaphysical suspension that his reading of Nietzsche had prompted on another level: the same mysterious incongruity of objects that were nonetheless symbolically associated. De Chirico himself later stated: "Böcklin, despite his infinite capacity for vision and evocation, was much more preoccupied than Klinger with all the technical problems of painting. In Klinger the pictorial question scarcely enters because all his creativity is based on the enormous possibilities of the exceptional spirit, the spirit of the poet, the philosopher, the observer, the dreamer, the scholar, the psychologist. In his work he has been, as a psychoanalyst, a sort of precursor of Sigmund Freud: in his depth and exceptional nature he has ties with Otto Weininger, and in a certain sense he may be compared with Picasso and our own [Italian] great Previati."

The Surrealists had sought to create a type of painting that clearly rejected cant: phrase-making on the light of a given landscape, disquisitions on "purely visible harmonies," happy recognition at sight of familiar objects arranged in familiar ways.

De Chirico, Savinio, and Metaphysical Painting

Breton never denied that De Chirico blazed the trail for the new art, nor did he stop affirming it in the succeeding editions of *Surrealism and Painting*. But he too bore a grudge against the great innovator bacause of his subsequent — never total — abandonment of Surrealism. Breton reaffirmed De Chirico's role in *Genesis and Perspectives*, published in 1941, praising the important paintings De Chirico had created in Milan, Turin, and Paris between 1912 and 1917.

Alberto Savinio was with his brother De Chirico in Paris at the time when Savinio's literary output began to take precedence over his music. (In the second half of the twenties painting at least briefly took precedence over his writing.) Toward the middle of the second decade, and therefore at the time when De Chirico was painting some of his most important canvases, Savinio's literary output was rich in witty sallies, in imagery, and even in Surrealist techniques.

And toward the end of the second decade, De Chirico wrote the sharpest and most lively declarations of metaphysical poetics, emphasizing especially that "Schopenhauer and Nietzsche were the first to teach the profound meaning of the non-sense of life and how that non-sense can be transmuted into art, in fact must constitute the inner skeleton of a truly new, free and profound art."

Italian Metaphysical painting, and particularly that of De Chirico and the works of Carrà between 1916 and 1920, marks the first affirmation of superreal painting in the dream sense. It had decisive consequences for a new generation of Surrealist painters, yet there is more than a little difference in the image in Metaphysical painting and in Surrealism: in the first, recourse to the technical aid of psychic automatism is sensed but not provoked, much less treated as a fetish. The determining moment is that of revelation which comes through an unexpected break in the logical lines of reality, a sort of loss of memory (which happens, according to Schopenhauer, to the mad), with the subsequent discovery of "new aspects and new spectral capacities." Surrealism, instead, invokes logically incongruous associations of revelatory images by the use of automatism. It does not, then, tend toward contemplation so much as toward *provocation* of reactions, actually psychic chain revelations. Inevitably, too, Surrealism has aspects of unbridled visionary quality and of black humor, which Metaphysical painting knew nothing of since it ignored the work of Freud.

8

Peter Selz, in *Seven Decades*, has defined the intention of Surrealism as that of "penetrating to the artists' innermost visions by suspending topical processes as much as possible. The sources of vision spring deep in the subjective unconscious—the dream, fantasy, hallucination. [The painters] demonstrate the magical experience of objects and dreams in juxtaposition, using that essential tool of artistic expression, the metaphor."

In Tzara's 1918 *Manifesto,* the artist made it clear that he believes automatism alone might free the imagination, and André Breton echoes the belief in his 1924 *Manifesto of Surrealism.* Breton writes of automatism: "Put yourself in as passive, or receptive, a state of mind as you can. Forget about your genius, your talents, the talents of everyone else....Write quickly, without any preconceived subject, fast enough so that you will not remember what you're writing and be tempted to reread what you've written...go on as long as you like....If silence threatens to settle in—break off without hesitation." Later on he adds, "I carefully refrain from starting over or polishing. The only thing that might prove fatal to me would be the slightest loss of impetus." So much for primarily verbal, poetic, Surrealism—the main subject of the 1924 *Manifesto.*

In 1929, sensing the roused tensions of a Europe once more headed for the holocaust, Breton drafted a second *Manifesto,* which was a sort of mise en point of the period. He wrote: "Surrealism attempted to provoke, from the intellectual and moral point of view, *an attack of conscience* of the broadest and most serious kind...the extent to which this was or was not accomplished alone can determine its historical success or failure." When Breton wrote these words it must have seemed a long time since he and many of the main figures of Dadaism had ventured toward a newer though no less revolutionary form of expression. The outstanding figures of Dadaism—Duchamp, Arp, Miró, Man Ray— followed their own path of nonfigurative painting right into the Surrealist movement. Many, however, feeling that their day of innovation was done or that they had personal grudges against Breton, Picasso, Duchamp, Ernst, broke with Surrealism in its middle years or were read out of it because of certain near libelous statements for which they had been responsible.

Picasso responded to Breton's rallying cry, saying that in the visual arts the so-called real values must be totally revised in the sense of interior reality or cease to have any validity. His painting had constantly undergone profound changes in an effort to achieve such a rendering of interior values and during his Cubist period Breton had written him: "You have left a rope ladder dangling from each painting, or even a dropcord of knotted sheets from each bedpost, and it is likely that all of us will climb down it or go up it in our sleep."

Meanwhile, Duchamp, in 1912, produced his epoch-making *Nude Descending a Staircase,* surely the most complete and free expression of visual movement the Futurists had articulated. Breton wrote at the time that the Italians had given to the Western world "a state of mind...in which art responded exclusively to need, to the task in hand," that is, they had made it possible to add the dimension of movement to the model, thus freeing this always *ex*teriorized subject (in contrast to the later Dadaists) from the binding restraints of immobility and conferring on it visual freedom.

In 1913 and 1914 many, if not most, of the French and Spanish painters sought whenever possible to avoid military involvement. More aware, or perhaps less subjectively involved than the Italians, some members emigrated to Switzerland or, among the non-French nationals, went to Spain or Portugal. It was a period of strange psychic pressures in which those painters who avoided the war seem to have been driven to produce at the top of their talent and energy. Marcel Jean, in his important *History of Surrealist Painting* (1959), called attention to the strongly exciting matter Duchamp elicited from banality: the ready-mades, the displacement of everyday objects by striking breaks and juxtapositions, the basic revelations of an unusual personality through its visions of pseudo-mechanical and often pseudo-scientific things. "The important thing here is that the viewer's attention has been shifted from the object to man....One soon lets oneself go in contemplation of the gracefulness of a great modern legend in which a lyrical quality unifies all" (Breton).

In 1918 Duchamp, whose bases of operations were Paris and New York, painted his great canvas *Tu m'* (Plate 7), saying of it: "This is a dictionary of the chief themes that preceded 1918, the 'ready-mades,' samples of cloth and of thread, receding shadows, use of distance," all brought together by a kind of automatism and spontaneity. The result had a quality of intensè lyricism not far from his *La Mariée*, but it was markedly less ironical.

Picabia's "mechanistic" paintings, all of which were characterized by the same type of vivid irony, had been started as early as 1914-15, and kept to the theme of the human image transformed mechanistically by its relations with its own surroundings. At the start of the next decade Picabia concentrated his lively imagination on the technique of collage: he used all sorts of media, feathers, matches and match-boxes, toothpicks, thread,and bits of tape measure to create landscapes, portraits, or fantastic versions of the human figure. In the mid-twenties this versatile painter started working with dream images, many of them monstrous (people with six eyes, creatures that were part serpent, and so on), and from there he passed on to more lyrical and defined though still largely abstract forms in the 1930s and 1940s.

Man Ray we naturally associate with Duchamp since the latter's visit to the United States in 1915. He was painting in the manner of the late Cubists when he met the French painter. Later he started experimenting with airbrush and created his famous Rayogrammes. Man Ray's passion for new media was to lead him into photography and film, yet he managed not to abandon painting or the creation of curious "objects." In fact it was he to whom the Surrealists owed many of the most creative and inventive objects of their repertory.

Hans Arp and Sophie Täuber gave up the use of oil on canvas to dedicate themselves to the exploration of how far the artist would go in the use of paper and cloth in collage. Arp also emphasized many geometric shapes, ovoids, mobile allusions to the human form. He started working in wood and created his famous series of reliefs; then in the twenties he began concentrating on sculpture, working in superb free forms that have movement, elegance, and great imaginative lift to them.

Quite aside from what the movement owed to De Chirico in the evocation of dreams, to Duchamp, Picabia, Miró, Arp, or Man Ray because of their experimental solutions, to Paul Klee because of his (always partial) automatism, we can now recognize with the passage of time that the full flowering of Surrealism did not appear until Max Ernst's work. Ernst introduced metamorphic, demoniac dynamism in his collages and paintings, an element that was lacking in the great De Chirico's contemplative style.

His smaller oils of the early period are often intermingled with collage and stress the mechanistic approach, almost downgrading the organic and physiological in a sinister fashion. The same holds true for his large paintings of the same period in which his rarefied use of space does recall De Chirico, paintings that feature dream images, creatures in a state of decomposition, day-to-day images juxtaposed in hallucinatory combinations. Toward the end of the twenties, Ernst moved away from the metaphysical use of space and began his period of concentration on geological and histological sections. It was in the late twenties and thirties that he began to insert concrete objects into his work. In the thirties too Max Ernst painted ever more broadly and productively, giving free rein to his visionary imagination, evoking demons, creatures of evil that seemed to foretell the madness and horror Hitler was to unleash on the world. He also used the decalcomania technique, which Oscar Domínguez had discovered, adding it to painting in oil.

The Belgian Leaders

Brussels was the home of René Magritte, the liveliest and most imaginative painter among the Belgian Surrealists. It was he, helped by the forward drive of E. L. T. Mesens, Camille Goemans, Van Hecke-Norine, and Paul Nougé among others who opened the Belgian gallery-goers' eyes to the new vision. (Admittedly, the small number of Surrealism's defenders in Belgium had to make up in enthusiasm for what they lacked in size.) "Everything Magritte paints is recognizable....It is the special way in which the parts are assembled that gives [them] a new identity," says Patrick Waldberg. Burning chairs, musical instruments; a cool white torso, chair, and tuba against a cloudless sky; dour figures walking from each other in theatric stillness along a beach strewn with scraps of cloud, such are the subjects that caught and held the viewer's attention. Magritte's work was published in *Oesophage*, in *Marie*, and he had close friendships among the writers who founded *Correspondance* in 1924.

Magritte felt that, by 1927, it was time for him to make direct contact with Breton and the artists who had grouped themselves about him. His fellow artists in Brussels evidently agreed with him for that year he left for Paris with their blessing. There his geniality, infectious humor—so apparent in the straight-faced, outrageous juxtapositions that characterize much of his work—his technical skill, and the evident (yet never labored) seriousness with which he took his work and that of the movement, quickly made him a personality of note. He stayed three years that time and wrote his important statement *La Révolution Surréaliste* in Paris in 1929. True to the mandate he had received from his fellow Belgians, he returned to Brussels in 1930 and set about cross-pollination with the Bretonists. The result was rich with highly imaginative work.

Magritte was far more important to Western painting than simply as a link between two major Surrealist groups. His work revealed exceptional variety in its imaginative solutions of pictorial problems. He worked against backgrounds of unrivaled richness, and he had his own highly characteristic moments of pure, lyric inventiveness (see particularly the great canvases of the late twenties such as *Polar Light*, or *The Relics of the Shadow*, Plates 25 and 26).

Ten years after Magritte's emergence, another Belgian leader of Surrealism entered the scene, Paul Delvaux. Only a year younger than Magritte, his thematic line from that day to this is the constant presence of the feminine image. Paul-Aloise de Bock has carefully reconstructed the origins of this theme of undisputed feminine dominance in the role of Delvaux's mother over the young painter—terror of womankind: her satanic projection, which is at the same time virginal, angelic; her distance, her untouchability. The terror ends when Delvaux, in his paintings, raises an altar to "beautiful womankind," offering the world this superior, impassive, apparently emotionless being on a pedestal (*Break of Day*, Plate 32).

The great erotic, vitalizing, and possessive cyclone that rushes through contemporary art is opposed by Delvaux's counterpoint of frustrated, impotent, nonpossessive eroticism (*Phases of the Moon*, Plate 33). He takes us back to the very first steps of psychotic disturbance: his world has no human couples, no warmth, no relatedness. People move in counterpoint and evoke a thematic balance predicated on distance from the possible love object. The symbolic use of props (the vase, the cushion, the broken column, the single flower) recalls those fixed (but often sunlit) standard elements of the world around De Chirico: the Greek or Roman landscape, the train, the streetcar.

Surrealism in Czechoslovakia

Given the time lag from East to West and, in these last centuries since we have had "manifested thoughts" to export, from West to East, it is not surprising that the Czech Surrealist movement was not formally constituted until 1934. Among the founders were the painters Styrsky, Toyen, and the sculptor Makovsky, the writers Nezval, Heisler, and Teige.

The paradoxical thing is that, two years before there was a constituted Czech Surrealism, the great free city of Prague had welcomed Surrealist painters, sculptors, artists of all kinds, to take part in one of the milestone gatherings of the movement, the international exposition *Poésie 1932*. Paul Eluard, ubiquitous red eminence of Communist Party official art, and André Breton, Surrealism's magic-voiced town crier, were given all possible official and unofficial honors as they brought the legitimizing force of their presences to the gathering.

But the Czech art world had been involved in the Surrealist exploration well before that, as early as ten years before. The paintings of Kupka and Preisler attest to a native "symbolist" tradition, and their influence was one of the formative elements of it. Another was the introduction of a dreamlike interpretation of nature, as seen in Zrzary's work. Then there was, inevitably, the important influence of the Cubist experience. These three, and more, were at work in Prague during the first stages to create the climate propitious to the "official" Surrealism of the thirties.

Moving on from the initial pictorial expressions of the earliest period, Jindrich Styrsky and Toyen proposed further exploration of the dream world in the form of lyric abstraction, or Artificialism, whose manifesto they had released as early as 1927. At the same time, Josef Sima furthered his investigations of dreams by painting lyric evocations of phantomlike images (*The Crow*, 1927, Plate 43).

Styrsky, enthusiastic from the first about the subtleties, paradoxes, and innovations of Surrealism in all its forms, illustrated the work of Lautreamont in 1928. This experience helped him discover a style that might be called "the dimensions of metamorphosis," and which came to characterize his paintings and drawings from the early thirties on, as they did those of his companion Toyen. Styrsky and Toyen at first recorded psychic reactions and what might be called imaginative analogues or parallels, the sort of "revelations" that characterized "artificialism." Then they went on to true Surrealist imagery, a highly personal, intimate, metamorphic, almost supernatural imagery that was all their own and which they preferred to the use of already depicted images (*Cigarette near a Corpse*, Plate 45, by Styrsky, and *At a Certain Hour*, Plate 46, by Toyen, are typical of their work). Styrsky's painting strikes a highly dramatic, often tragic note, while that of Toyen is more mobile in its passage from darkly dramatic to subtly lyric expression. Even today Toyen's imaginative creation remains extremely rich in varied themes yet always highly personal.

Surrealism in Other Countries of Western Europe

Active Surrealist groups sprang up in many countries, among them Rumania, whose best-known artist was Victor Brauner. After a couple of years spent in

Paris, Brauner returned to act as the lode star of the Rumanian branch of the movement between 1935 and 1938. (He went back to France in 1938.)

Brauner concentrated first on dream visions of horrendous power and violence (his so-called Chimera period), distortions reminiscent of the little Bosch monsters of the Escurial *Triptych*, creatures—or rather creations—which, as Elie Faure says, communicate "the secret misery of nature." In the forties he moved on to paint magical archetypes of great emotional power. "His work," says Waldberg, "is a speculation on the conjuring power of the image." One of his most striking works, *Myths at Large*, dating from 1945, is strangely reminiscent in coloration to the Aztec fresco-type tones of the clay-painting countries, while his composition and images have a poised loneliness and apparent lack of rationale that exude an eerie sense of the tragedy of alienated humanity. He continued to paint in this vein until his death in 1966.

Among the Rumanians, Jacques Hérold must be remembered—although most Rumanian art lovers associate him more clearly with France than with his native land. Hérold went to Paris in 1930 and, for a little more than five years, painted metamorphic, evocative canvases of an increasingly depersonalized character. There were bands of muscles; detached and meticulously articulated "mosaics" in paint suggesting the human body; crystals; subtly fractured and fragmented minerals. Everywhere in his work are traces of his enduring preoccupation with materials and space. (*The Forest*, Plate 38.)

Proof that Surrealism did not exclude the far north is to be found in the work of Wilhelm Freddie of the Danish group. His first show, called Sex-Surreal, opened in Copenhagen in 1937 and was speedily closed by the police. In his perhaps therapeutic desire to shock, Freddie presented images that he called "sado-masochistic interiors," and "psycho-photographic phenomena." His attitude toward his viewers was frankly aggressive and would be considered so even today, the drive behind the manifestations ("objects" as well as paintings) being more or less explicitly to reduce his public to a moment of stunned awareness by the driving force of his (unwelcome) images.

North Europe since World War II has produced one outstanding new talent in the Swede Max Walter Svanberg. His use of erotic themes has produced a veritable paroxysm of decorative density and he seems, strangely, vitally related to the present while evoking the earlier Surrealist apogee.

Then there is the gigantic figure of Max Ernst, whose versatility, technical skill, taste, imagination, and seemingly eternal productivity has placed him at the very forefront of modern art. To tie Ernst's work to German Surrealism alone would be like giving geographical limitations to a torrent. But there he is, along with Hans Bellmer and Richard Oelze, the three most important personalities in the German Movement.

Surrealism in North America

In 1936 Alfred Barr organized an epoch-making exhibition in New York that

14

sparked research and further innovation on the part of American Surrealist painters. When, six years later, another important exhibit was organized, New York, among other localities in the United States, had had the toxin/anti-toxin advantage of Breton's presence, and that of many other European Surrealist painters who had emigrated to the United States. Among those who brought their distinct contributions to America were Max Ernst, Yves Tanguy, Marcel Duchamp, and André Masson.

· Nor were the European painters the only ones to contribute to the developmental stimulus at work in New York at this time. The Chilean Roberto Matta Echaurren (Matta) and the Cuban Wilfredo Lam joined forces with Robert Motherwell, one of the leaders of North American Abstract Expressionism in the second half of the 1940s. Among them they exercised startling impact on the younger American painters.

Matta's considerable fascination lay in the fact that he expressed a seemingly unquestioning belief in the "perfectibility of human faculties, and in man's limitless, only slightly derailed, capacity for invention, comprehension, and marvel-making," as Breton called it.

Lam's situation was very different; a highly charged background—Lam was part Chinese, part African—plus early recognition by Picasso, who encouraged the younger painter's drive to explore his Cuban ambience, *plus* the awareness and wariness of a true primitive toward the world around him combined to loose a furious, explosive talent on the world. In addition, Lam had achieved great technical skill. He turned these many attributes to the re-creation of his special atmosphere with its echoes of pre-historic Indian civilization, African ritual, and his own version of western European sophistication. This is a form of painting that carries the animistic-totemic echoes of the jungle within it, stressing the terrifying violence and cruelty that lie just below a surface of shimmering verdant fascination and apparent calm.

Most sensitive and original of the younger American painters of the period, Arshile Gorky at first reflected the influence of Cézanne, Matisse, and Picasso, and later that of Miró among the Europeans, and Matta among the South Americans. Called by W. S. Rubin "the last important artist to be associated with Surrealism," Gorky had been painting since adolescence. He had come to the United States from Armenia at the age of sixteen, studied at the Rhode Island School of Design, and, in deracination and loneliness, fought his continuing inward battle to achieve a style authentically his own. One of the apparently extraneous factors that contributed to Gorky's originality was his very love of oil paint. Unlike the major figures of the Dadaist and Surrealist movements, many of whom had gone out of their way to invent new techniques that often showed startling virtuosity, Gorky was happiest with the same medium that had satisfied the painters of the past.

Coming into his own in the early 1940s, this luminous, lyrical painter met with every sort of formal recognition from the European masters then in this country because of the war. Breton, who had recognized the significance of his work at once, wrote an important preface to his one-man show in 1945, and at last his work attracted enormous attention here and abroad. But two years later, in response to the implacable series of heartbreaking tragedies that had struck him and his family, Gorky hanged himself at his home in Sherman, Connecticut. One of his last works, *Agony*, shows, as Patrick Waldberg says, that "wholly personal sensibility, that quivering grace of a frightened bird" that lent poignant beauty to his works.

Of course, it is no more possible here to give a full account of Surrealism in America than it is to cover the movement's ramifications over the globe. The main fact is that Surrealism contributed directly to the development of Abstract Expressionism. Proto-Surrealism, with its emphasis on automatism, strongly influenced Jackson Pollock in the latter half of the forties and his uses of it were completely personal and subjective.

The forces of Surrealism worked especially on the imaginations of those painters and sculptors drawn to the movement—from the 1920s to the 1950s. In the history of art experience, any influence that extends from Dada to Pop must have some enduring element of vitality. The Surrealist heritage still stands as a vital force because it has opened windows on a new view of the world.

PLATES

De Chirico

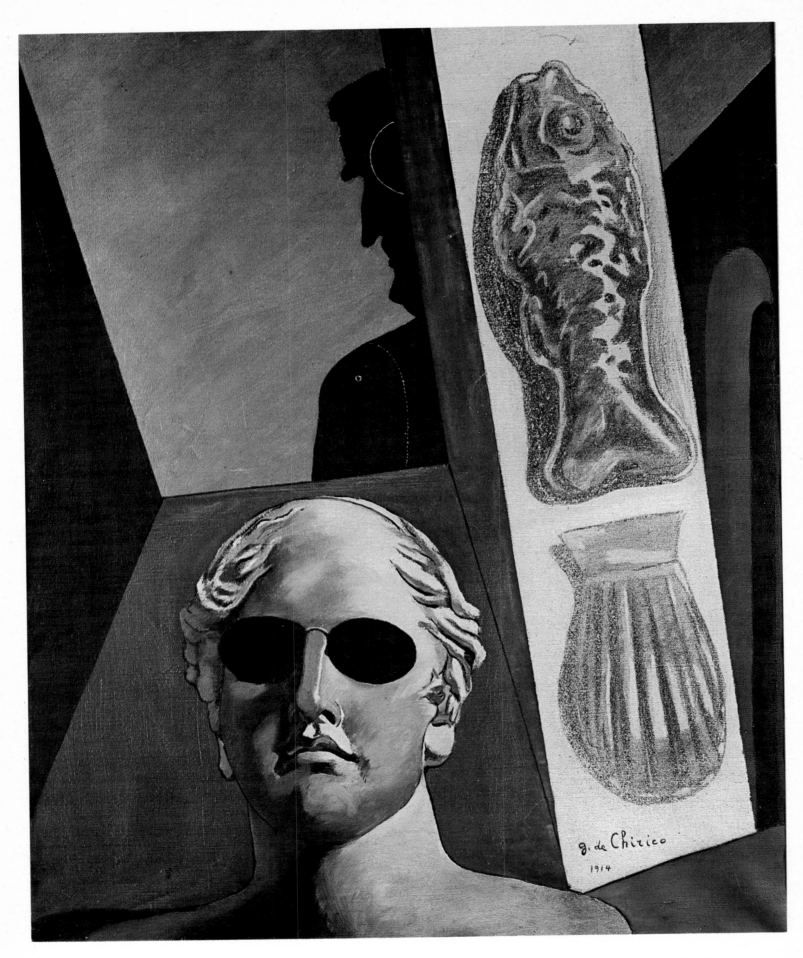

PLATE 2 Giorgio de Chirico *Portrait of Guillaume Apollinaire,* 1914 (85 x 78 cm) Paris, private collection

PLATE 3 GIORGIO DE CHIRICO *La Piazza d'Italia*, 1915 (51 x 64 cm) Rome, private collection

PLATE 4 FRANCIS PICABIA *Feathers*, 1921 (119 x 78 cm) Milan, Galleria Schwarz

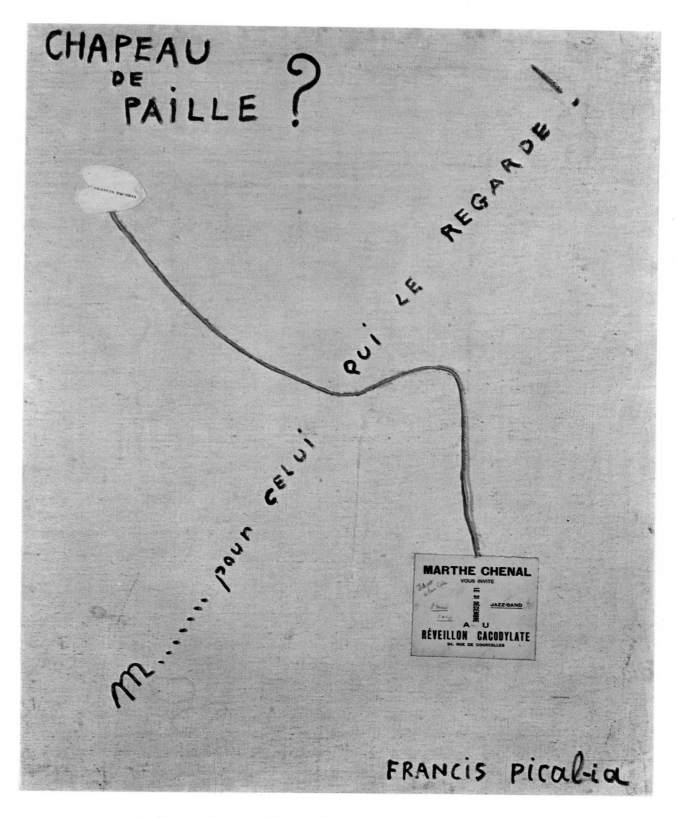

PLATE 5 FRANCIS PICABIA *Chapeau de Paille*, 1921, Paris, Dr. Le Masle Collection

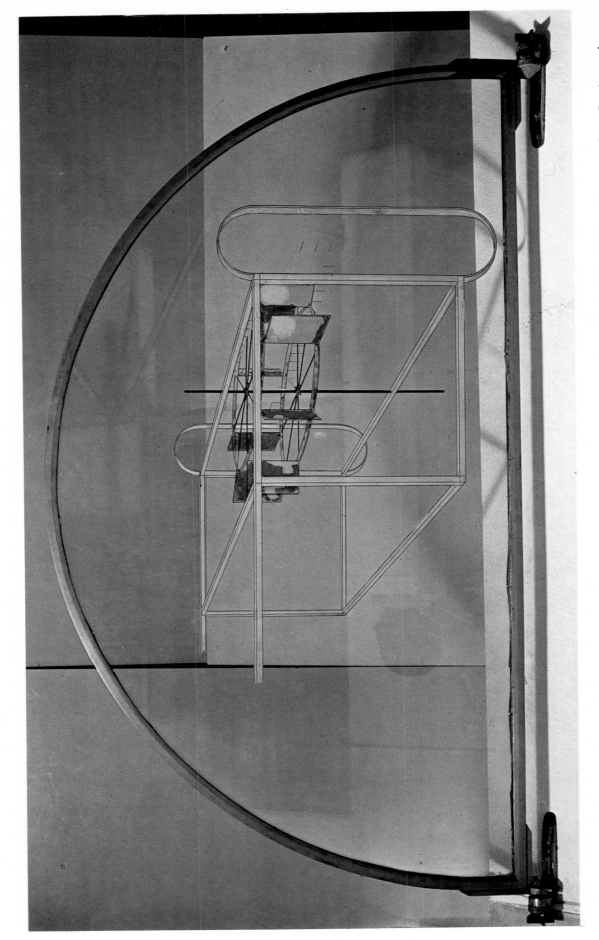

PLATE 6 MARCEL DUCHAMP *Glider Containing a Water Mill in Neighboring Metals,* 1913–15 (79 x 147 cm) Philadelphia, Museum of Art, Louise and Walter Arensberg Collection

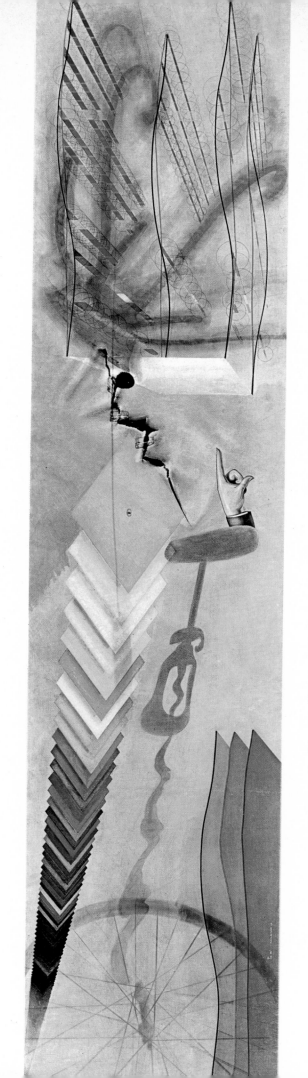

PLATE 7   MARCEL DUCHAMP *Tu m'*, 1918 (70 x 313 cm) New Haven, Yale University Art Gallery

PLATE 8 HANS ARP *Fork and Shirtfront,* 1924 (50 x 57 cm) Liège, Fernand Graindorge Collection

26

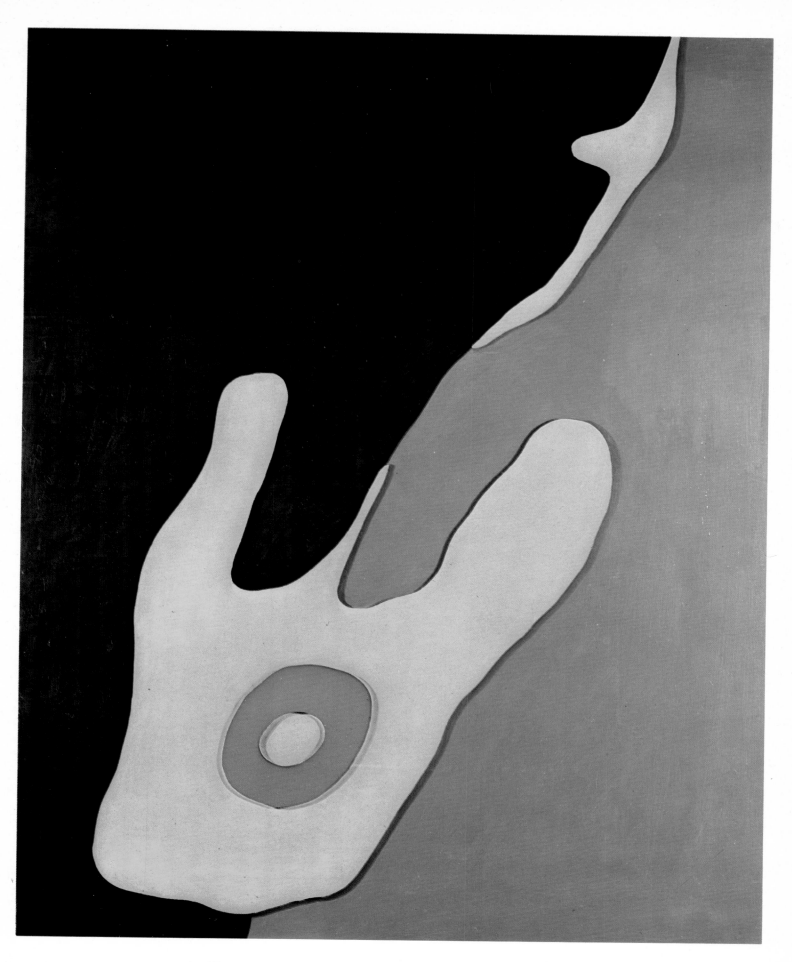

PLATE 9 HANS ARP *Configuration*, 1927–28 (145 x 115.5 cm) Basel, Kunstmuseum

PLATE 10   MAN RAY *Legend,* 1916 (131 x 91 cm) Brussels, Urvater Collection

28

Ernst, Masson, Miró, Tanguy, Magritte

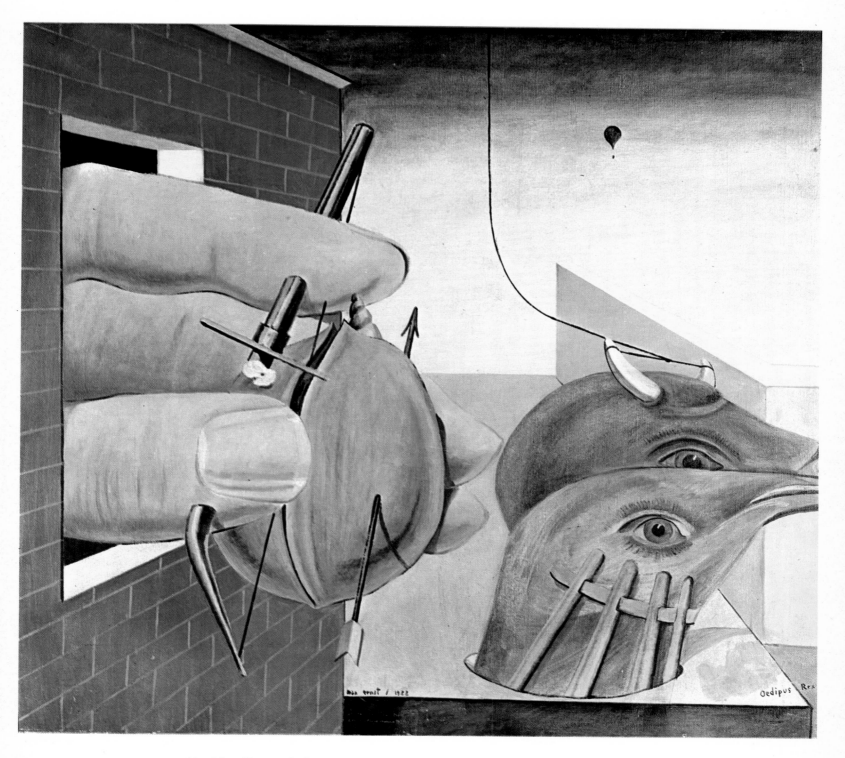

PLATE 11　MAX ERNST *Oedipus Rex*, 1922 (93 x 102.2 cm) Paris, Claude Hersaint Collection

PLATE 12   MAX ERNST *Headless Figures,* 1928 (162 x 130 cm) Milan, Ezy Nahmad Collection

PLATE 13   MAX ERNST *Sunset*, 1929 (100 x 80 cm) Milan, Franco Zerbi Collection

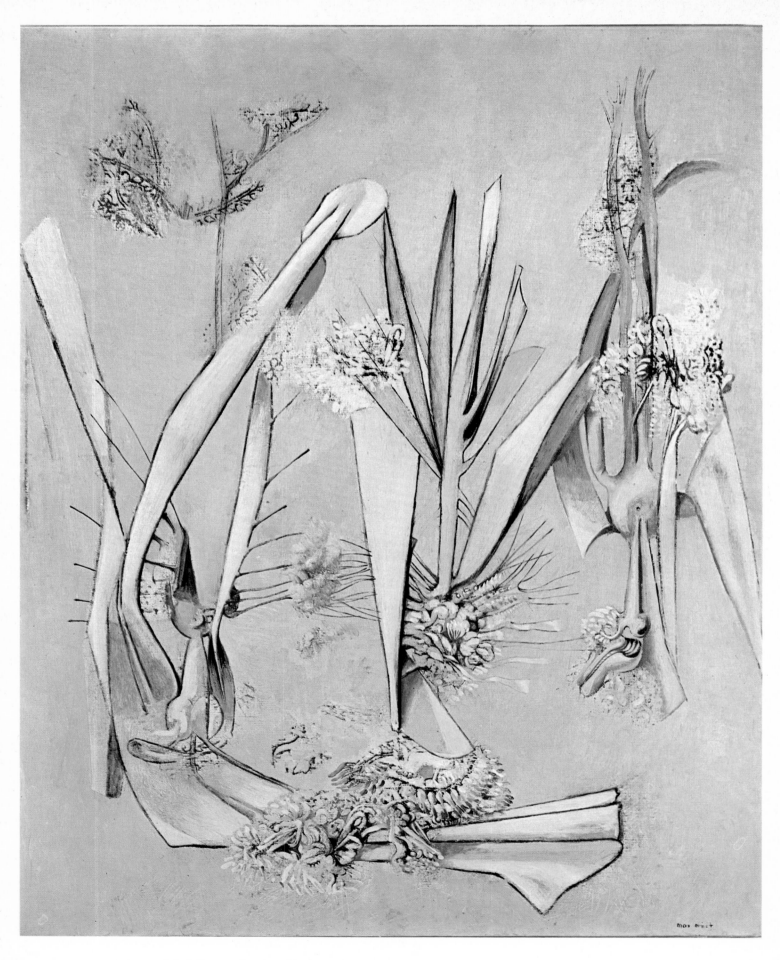

PLATE 14   MAX ERNST *Garden Airplane Trap*, 1935 (81 x 65 cm) Brussels, Jean Dypréau Collection

PLATE 15   ANDRÉ MASSON *The Mélusine Sisters*, 1958 (50 x 65 cm) Paris, Galerie Louise Leiris

PLATE 16   ANDRÉ MASSON *The Fig,* 1924 (65 x 50 cm) Paris, Simone Collinet Collection

PLATE 17 YVES TANGUY *Death Eying His Family with Suspicion*, 1927, Paris, Jéramec Collection

PLATE 18   JOAN MIRÓ *Seated Woman II,* 1939 (160 x 129 cm) Venice, Peggy Guggenheim Collection

PLATE 19 JOAN MIRÓ *Portrait of Mistress Mills in 1750*, 1929 (116 x 89 cm) New Canaan, Conn., James T. Soby Collection

PLATE 20   JOAN MIRÓ *Woman in the Night,* 1967 (132 x 108 cm) Milan, private collection

PLATE 21   JOAN MIRÓ *Personage* (70 x 100 cm) Milan, private collection

PLATE 22 YVES TANGUY *Multiplication of Arcs,* 1954 (101.6 x 152.4 cm) New York, Museum of Modern Art, Mrs. Simon Guggenheim Fund

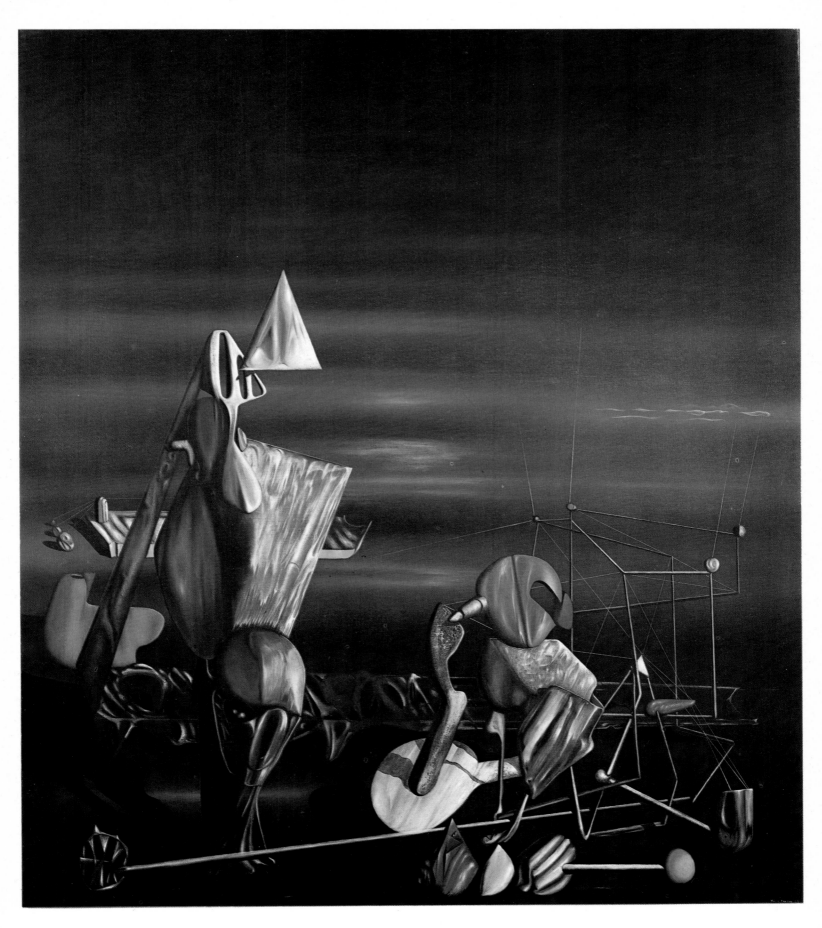

PLATE 23   YVES TANGUY *Slowly Toward the North*, 1942 (106 x 91.4 cm) New York, Museum of Modern Art

PLATE 24   YVES TANGUY *The Day I Shall Be Shot*, 1927 (106 x 86 cm) Milan, private collection

PLATE 25 RENÉ MAGRITTE *Polar Light,* 1927 (138 x 104 cm) Rome, Ponti-Loren Collection

PLATE 26 RENÉ MAGRITTE *The Relics of the Shadow* (120 x 80 cm) Grenoble, Musée des Beaux-Arts

PLATE 27   RENÉ MAGRITTE *The Chair*, 1950 (60 x 50 cm) Rome, private collection

PLATE 28 GIORGIO DE CHIRICO *The Trophy,* 1926 (100 x 75 cm) Milan, Laurini Collection

PLATE 29   ALBERTO SAVINIO *The Night of Solomon*, 1930 (65 x 55 cm) Milan, Laurini Collection

PLATE 30   ALBERTO SAVINIO *Carpophagus Awakening*, 1930 (73 x 92 cm) Rome, private collection

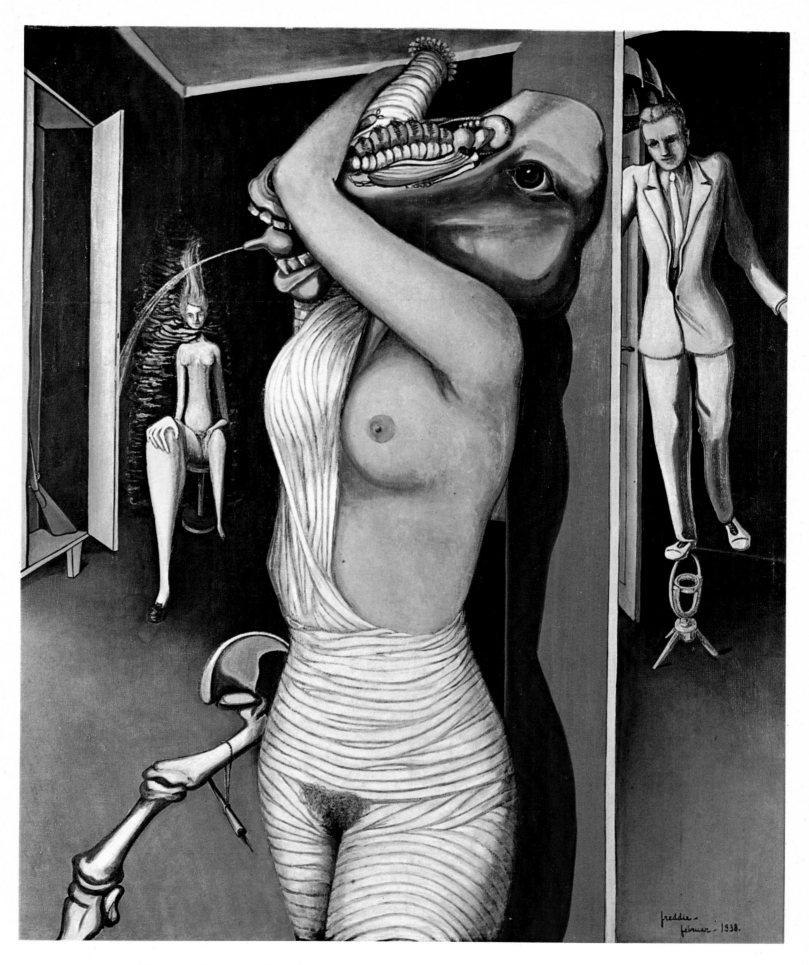

PLATE 31   WILHELM FREDDIE *Zola and Jeanne Rozerot*, 1938 (100 x 83 cm) Copenhagen, Jörn Freddie Collection

PLATE 32   PAUL DELVAUX *Break of Day*, 1937 (120 x 150 cm) Venice, Peggy Guggenheim Collection

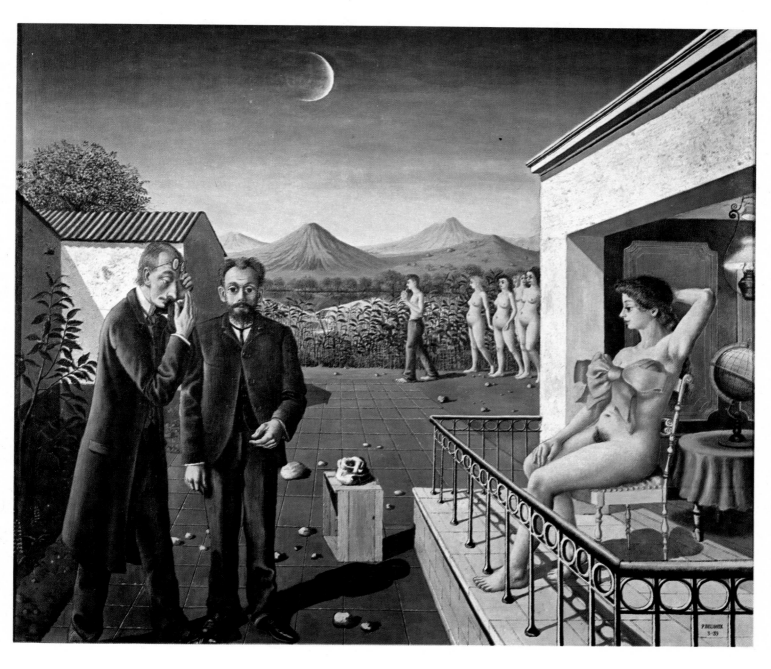

PLATE 33   PAUL DELVAUX *Phases of the Moon*, 1939 (139.7 x 160 cm) New York, Museum of Modern Art

PLATE 34 MAX WALTER SVANBERG *Chimera*, 1953 (65 x 51 cm) Paris, Breton Collection

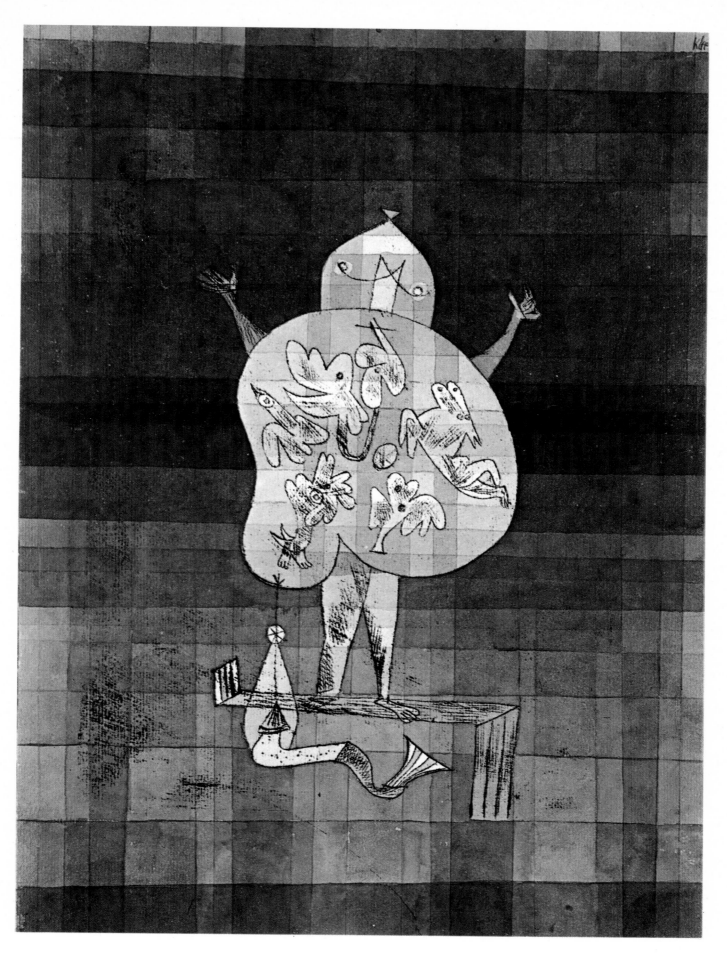

PLATE 35   PAUL KLEE *The Ventriloquist and Caller on the Moor,* 1923 (41 x 29 cm) Paris, Heinz Berggruen Collection

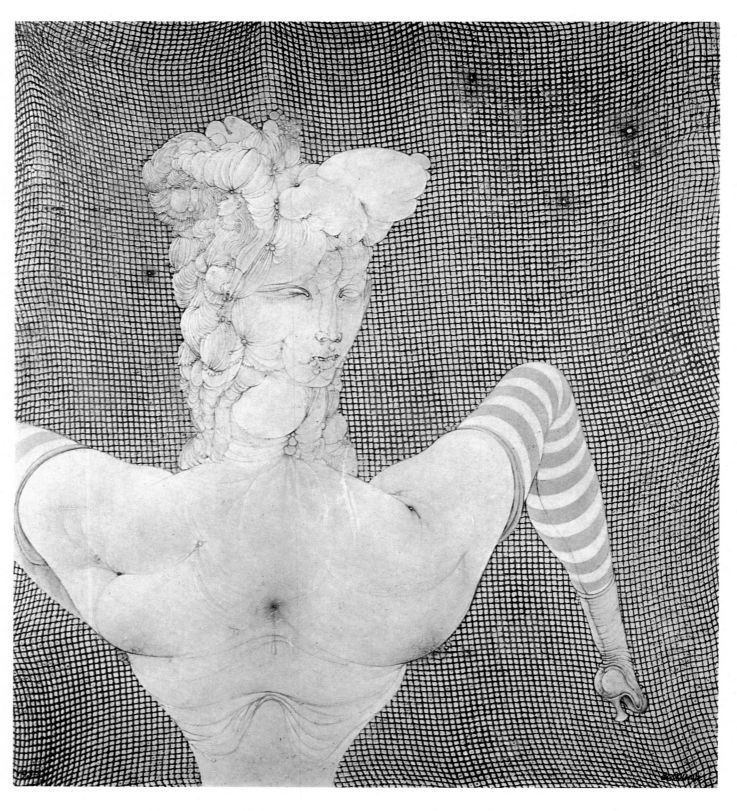

PLATE 36   HANS BELLMER *Iridescent Cephalopod,* 1939 (49 x 44 cm) Paris, Galerie Francois Petit

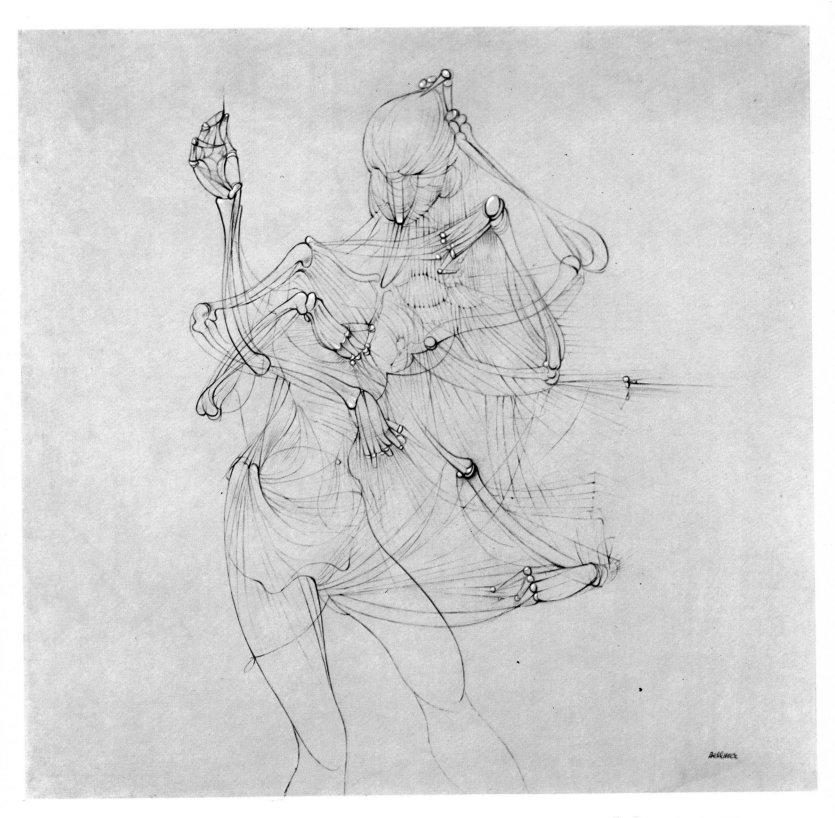

PLATE 37   HANS BELLMER *Woman with Articulated Arms,* 1965 (65 x 65 cm) Rome, Studio d'Arte Condotti 85

PLATE 38   JACQUES HÉROLD *The Forest,* 1945 (46 x 33 cm) Paris, private collection

PLATE 39   PABLO PICASSO *Figures at the Seashore,* 1931 (130 x 195 cm) private collection

PLATE 40   RICHARD OELZE *Small Landscape,* c. 1935 (13 x 17 cm) formerly in the Joe Bousquet Collection

PLATE 41   SIMON HANTAI *Composition*, 1952 (93 x 111.5 cm) Paris, Marcel Nahmias Collection

PLATE 42   OSCAR DOMÍNGUEZ *The Safety Pin,* 1937 (60 x 49 cm) Milan, Galleria Milano

PLATE 43   JOSEPH SIMA *Crow*, 1927 (130 x 70 cm) Paris, Galerie Le Point Cardinal

PLATE 44   JOSEPH SIMA *Untitled,* 1933 (130 x 88 cm) Prague, Narodni Galerie

PLATE 45   JINDRICH STYRSKY *Cigarette near a Corpse,* 1931 (94 x 135 cm) Ostrava, Czechoslovakia, Galerie Ostrava

PLATE 46 TOYEN *At a Certain Hour,* 1963 (49 x 39 cm) Paris, Guy Flandre Collection

PLATE 47   TOYEN *Wake in a Mirror,* 1959 (130 x 81 cm) Paris, collection of the artist

65

PLATE 48   Frantisek Janousek *Images,* 1939 (62 x 78 cm) Prague, private collection

PLATE 49   JOSEPH ISTLER *Ecstasy*, 1951 (235 x 143 cm) Prague, private collection

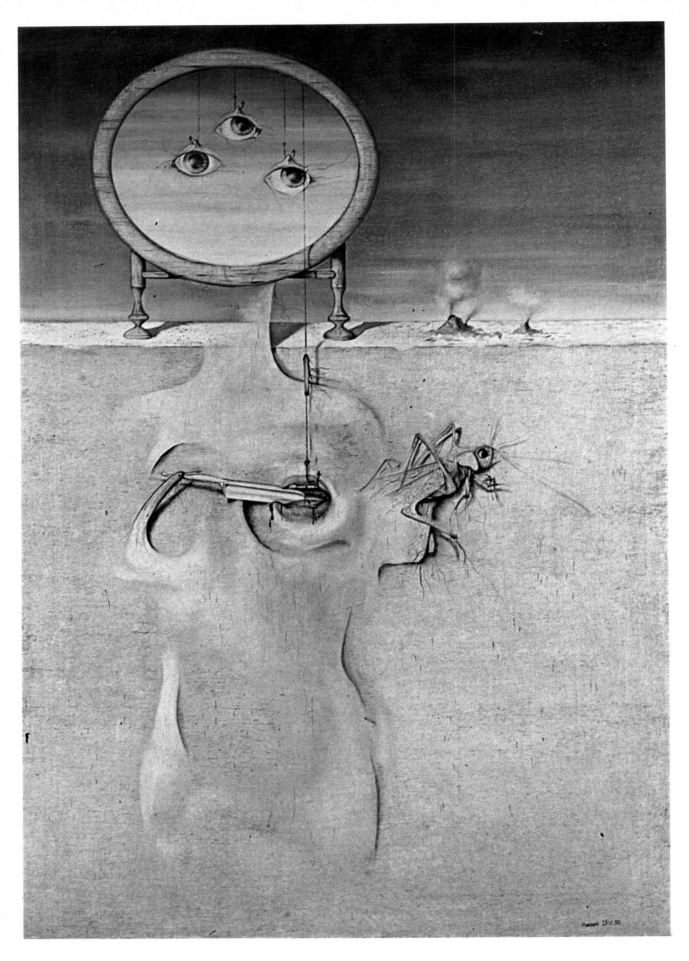

PLATE 50 MIKULÁS MEDEK *Sounds of Silence,* 1950 (120 x 82 cm) Prague, private collection

PLATE 51   FRANTISEK MUZIKA *Theater II,* 1944 (80 x 100 cm) Hluboka, Czechoslovakia, Galerie Ales

PLATE 52   ARSHILE GORKY *Landscape Table*, 1945 (93.9 x 124.4 cm) New York, B. H. Friedman Collection

PLATE 53   ARSHILE GORKY *Garden in Sochi,* 1941 (78 x 99 cm) New York, Gorky Estate

PLATE 54 WOLFGANG PAALEN *Battle of the Saturnian Princes,* 1938 (100 x 73 cm) Paris, Jacques Tronche Collection

PLATE 55   MAX ERNST *Day and Night,* 1943 (111.7 x 144.7 cm) New Orleans, Dr. and Mrs. Richard W. Levy Collection

PLATE 56   WIFREDO LAM *Figure*, 1938 (100 x 75 cm) Paris, collection of the artist

PLATE 57   WIFREDO LAM *Jungle*, 1944 (93 x 74 cm) Paris, private collection

PLATE 58   MATTA *Toward Alisma,* 1948 (148 x 132 cm) Paris, Galerie du Dragon

PLATE 59   MATTA *Psychological Morphology,* 1938 (73 x 92 cm) private collection

PLATE 60   ANDRÉ MASSON *Iriquois Landscape,* 1943 (76 x 100 cm) Paris, Simone Collinet Collection

THE ARTISTS

HANS ARP

Born in Strasbourg, September 16, 1887. He studied in Weimar and Paris and, in 1911, together with Helbig and Lüthy, he founded "Der moderne Bund" (The Modern Group). A few years later he worked with them again in Zurich, where they were associated with Tzara in the Dadaist movement of which Arp became the chief exponent. In 1913 he met Max Ernst in Cologne. The previous year he had shown his work at The Blue Rider Gallery, thanks to Kandinsky. During this period he illustrated many Dadaist literary works with woodcuts and drawings. In 1919 he was one of the leaders of the group of "radical artists" whose tendency was definitely abstract. Arp was also a prolific and important poet.

During the twenties Arp created his famous reliefs. In 1925 he took part in the first Surrealist exposition; the next year he went to settle in Meudon near Versailles and Paris. In the following decades, until his death in 1966 in Basel, his chief artistic medium was sculpture.

ARP *Large Figure*, 1960, private collection

BELLMER *Drawing*, (62 x 47 cm) Rome, Studio d'Arte Condotti 85

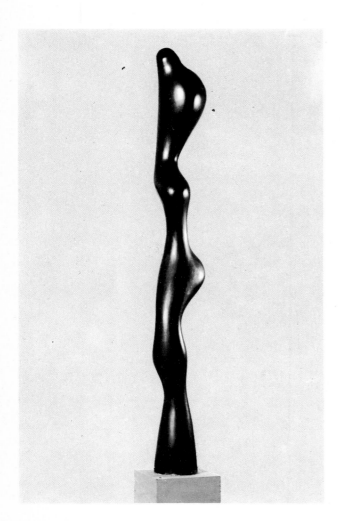

HANS BELLMER

Born in Katowice, Poland, March 13, 1902. In Berlin, where he worked as a graphic artist for an advertising firm, he knew Grosz, Heartfield, and Schlichter, who introduced him to Dadaism.

And in 1924–25, during a trip to Paris, he discovered the work of Pascin.

In 1933 Bellmer began to work on *The Doll*, a provocative, erotic wooden manikin, photographs of which appeared in 1935 in *The Minotaure* under the title *Variations on Mounting an Articulated Minor*. They had been published in book form the previous year. The French edition of the book, published in 1936, brought Bellmer into contact with Eluard, Breton, and Tanguy. In 1937 he moved to Paris, where he still lives. During the German occupation he had to flee Nazi persecution. In 1949 he and Eluard collaborated on a book, *The Doll's Games*, and in 1957 he published an analysis of his own creative processes, *Short Anatomy of the Psychic Unconscious or the Anatomy of the Image.*

SALVADOR DALI

Born in Figueras, near Barcelona, Spain, May 11, 1904. He studied at the Academy of Fine Arts in Madrid. The metaphysical painting of de Chirico first impressed him in 1924 and he discovered Surrealism the next year, perhaps influenced by Tanguy's first works reproduced in *The Minotaure*. In Madrid he belonged to the group of avant-garde intellectuals that included Garcia Lorca and Bunuel, and he collaborated with the latter in 1928 on the film *Un chien andalou*. He had an important one-man show in Paris in 1929. In 1930 he published *The Visible Woman*, in which he theorized on the "critico-paranoid method" of painting.

A decade later he moved to New York, where, in 1942, he published *The Secret Life of Salvador Dali*. After World War II, he returned to Spain, where he lived in Cadaqués for several years. Because of

DE CHIRICO *Lithograph for Jean Cocteau's "Mythology,"* 1934

his reactionary political sympathies he was repudiated by the Surrealist group.

He now lives and works in New York.

GIORGIO DE CHIRICO

Born in Greece, July 10, 1888, at Volos in Thessaly. He is the older brother of Alberto Savinio (*see page 88*). He began his studies at Athens Polytechnic and went on to the Academy of Fine Arts in Munich. He visited Milan in 1909 and the next year went to Florence. In 1911 de Chirico moved to Paris, following a visit to Turin, where he was impressed by the characteristics of the city, as Nietzsche had been before him. After a period of direct influence by Böcklin, his own "metaphysical" painting emerged between 1910 and 1911. Between 1912 and 1914 he created several masterpieces based on the major theme of the Italian

While the metaphysical school was expanding to include poetry, de Chirico started painting manikins, then interiors and still lifes. In 1918 he went to live in Rome and underwent a change that led him to abandon his early Surrealist style. In the twenties and thirties his work continued to change constantly under the influence of intensely personal mythological evocations or Surrealist visions. He did not really break away from his search for the contemporaneous into an academic Baroque style until after World War II. Recently he has returned to painting metaphysical themes with fresh enthusiasm. These are not at all cold echoes and derivations of his earlier work, as in past decades, but paintings full of pictorial felicity.

In 1920 Giorgio de Chirico, the friend of Apollinaire, sought after by Tzara, idolized by André Breton and the Surrealists (on whom he had a

profound influence), had a sharp break with the group—except Paul Eluard. The break with the Surrealists widened as the decade wore on. In 1929 he published in Paris a singular novel based on his own life, *Hebdomeros,* which spells out the record of his metaphysical painting.

He lives and works in Rome.

PAUL DELVAUX

Born in Huy, Belgium, September 23, 1897. His father was a lawyer, and Paul grew up in Brussels. First he studied the humanities, then he went to the Academy of Fine Arts. In 1924 he began to show his paintings, which were in a generally Post-Impressionist vein. It was not until 1934 that Delvaux had a revelation of his own imaginative tendencies when he discovered de Chirico and Surrealist painting at *The Minotaure* exposition, which took place that year at the Palace of Fine Arts in Brussels. In the years that immediately followed, his work aroused the interest of Eluard and Breton. In Paris in 1938, and again in Mexico City two years later, Delvaux showed with the Surrealists, although he remained largely autonomous. In fact, he accepted Surrealism

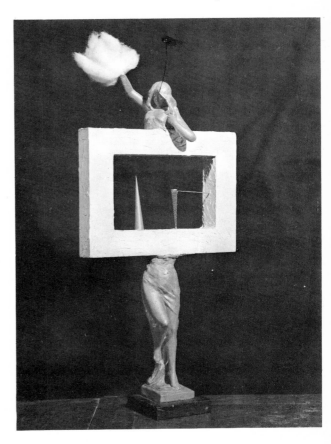

DOMÍNGUEZ *The Arrival of the Belle Epoque*, 1936, Paris, Marcel Jean Collection

especially as "the recrudescence of the poetic idea in art, the reintroduction of the subject, but in a clearly determined way, namely under a strange or illogical form." He was also specific at that time that "...it's quite another thing to be part of a movement."

From 1950 to 1962 he taught at the National

DUCHAMP *Pocket Chessboard*, 1943–44, Paris, private collection

Upper School of Art and Architecture in Brussels. In 1965 and 1966 he was president and director of the Royal Academy of Fine Arts in that city, where he currently resides.

OSCAR DOMINGUEZ

Born in Tacoron in the Canary Islands in 1906. In 1934 he joined the Surrealist movement, after having held a modest show of Surrealist work in Tenerife the year before. In 1935 he organized the famous Surrealist Exposition there and from then on took an official part in the exhibits of the group.

During World War II he stayed in France. He committed suicide in Paris in 1957.

MARCEL DUCHAMP

Born in Blainville, France, July 28, 1887. He was the brother of the sculptor Raymond Duchamp-Villon and of the painters Jacques Villon (Gaston Duchamp) and Suzanne Duchamp. As early as 1913–14 he began to use ready-made objects, more or less modified, which anticipated later Dadaist work. Along with Man Ray and Picabia, he went to New York in 1915, where the three promoted Dadaism. He returned to Paris in 1918 to develop further his own Dadaist activity. At the beginning of the 1920s he was painting in the Cubist and Futurist styles.

In 1922 he was once more in New York to complete work on his *Grand verre* (Big Glass), again returning to Paris in 1923, where he stayed until 1926. The publication of his *Green Box* recapitulates his creative activity in a sort of personal museum in miniature.

Duchamp worked closely and actively with André Breton to organize the international Surrealist exhibitions of Paris (1938), New York (1942), Paris (1947), and again Paris (1959). He died in that city in 1968.

MAX ERNST

Born near Cologne, Germany, in 1891. He studied philosophy at the University of Bonn. The son of an amateur painter, he was self-taught in art. Once he had become acquainted with Macke, he began to paint in a visionary, Expressionist way close to the spirit generated by the Blue Rider group (*see* Arp). In 1913 he met Arp, and in 1919 he discovered the work of de Chirico. In 1920 he published *Die Schammade* in Cologne together with Baargeld, and with Arp he formed an active Dadaist group. In that same year André Breton discovered his Dadaist collages, and in 1922 Ernst moved to Paris. From 1921 on, his work as a Surrealist painter was particularly intense. He published his story-collages in the late 1920s and early 1930s, including *The Woman of 100 Heads, The Review of a Little Girl Who Wanted to Become a Carmelite*, and *One Week of Goodness*.

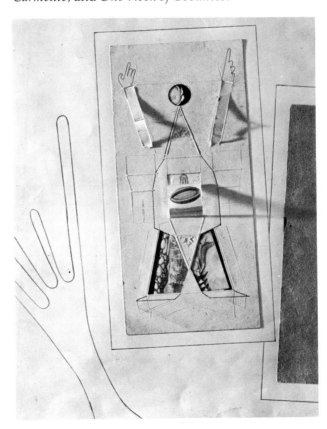

ERNST *Collage*, 1931, Paris, private collection

In 1938 Max Ernst took an active part in organizing the International Exposition of Surrealism in Paris. During the Nazi occupation of France he sought refuge in New York. In 1943 he settled in Sedona, Arizona, with Dorothea Tanning, where he worked intensively on sculpture. A decade later, he returned to France and settled near Chinon in Touraine. Having accepted the prize at the Venice Biennial of 1954, he was ousted by the Surrealist group.

He continues to be extraordinarily creative.

WILHELM FREDDIE

Born in Copenhagen, February 7, 1909. In 1930 he introduced Surrealism to Denmark and later fell under the influence of Dali. He exhibited in Surrealist shows in London and New York in 1936. The following year his one-man show in Copenhagen, entitled Sex-Surreal: Take the Fork Out of the Butterfly's Eye, drove the public to violent reactions. Some viewers even tried to strangle the painter, and the show was closed by the police. Two paintings and one piece of sculpture were seized and ended up at the Criminal Museum of Copenhagen.

His one-man shows of 1939 and 1940 in Copenhagen, and in Aarhus and Odensee in 1941, were also threatened by the police. When the Nazis occupied Denmark in 1940, Freddie was the target of a particularly vicious press campaign. Finally, in 1944, he sought refuge in Sweden and settled in Stockholm until 1950.

FREDDIE *Object*, Stockholm, Moderna Museet

In the post-World War II period Freddie's work continued to create intense interest, even in the fields of film and objects (he had created many objects in the thirties). He was a member of the Spiralen group in Copenhagen, and the group

GORKY *Drawing*, 1944 (49 x 63 cm) Paris, Galerie M. Knoedler

known as Phases, directed by Jaguer, in Paris. He now lives in Copenhagen.

ARSHILE GORKY

Born in Khorkom Vari Haiyotz Dzor, Armenia, in 1904, and came to the United States with his younger sister in 1920. He studied at the Rhode Island School of Design in Providence, and in Boston. In 1929 he met Stuart Davis, and in 1933, de Kooning. His first one-man show took place the following year. In this period Gorky was influenced by Picasso, and later by Miró.

The original qualities of his creative personality began to emerge in the forties. In 1944 he met Breton, who wrote the introduction to Gorky's important one-man show of the following year. Depressed over a series of misfortunes, the painter killed himself in 1948 in Sherman, Connecticut, where he had gone to live in 1945. His work represents the welding together of the Surrealist tradition and the Abstract Expressionism of North America.

SIMON HANTAI

Born in Bia, Hungary, in 1922. His Surrealist experiments began in the forties, extending into the fifties. In 1952 he came into direct contact with Breton, who introduced his one-man show in Paris the following year. In about 1955 Hantai began to seek increasingly automatic solutions of conceptualization in his painting. From that time on he collaborated with the French painter Georges Mathieu in work tending toward experiments in an informal, abstract lyricism.

JACQUES HÉROLD

Born in Piatra, Rumania, October 10, 1910. He studied at the Academy of Fine Arts in Bucharest and, in 1930, transferred to Paris. In 1934 he joined the Surrealist group for a short time, left it, then returned to it in the period from 1938 to 1951. He was always extremely active in the graphic arts and illustrated numerous literary works.

In 1957 Hérold published a collection of reflections on his life and art, a personal poetics called *Ill Treated by Painting.*

JOSEPH ISTLER

Born in Prague, November 13, 1919. He studied in Yugoslavia with Walter Hoefner. During the Nazi occupation he worked clandestinely to produce graphics of genuine importance, foretelling a kind of informal, abstract lyricism. At that time his general inclinations were toward giving form to the Surrealist imagination. Between 1946 and 1948, as a member of the Ra group, Istler participated in the revolutionary 1947 International Conference on Surrealism in Brussels and in the Cobra movement.

In the 1960s Joseph Istler was one of the leaders of Czech informal structural abstraction. He is now living in Prague.

FRANTISEK JANOUSEK

Born in Prague in 1890. Originally influenced by Miró and Dali (at the time he took part in the exhibit Poésie 1932), his work became more clearly individual in its shift toward tragic metamorphism in the second half of the 1930s.

Janousek was killed by the Nazis in 1943.

WILFRID LAM

Born in Sagua la Grande, Cuba, December 2, 1902. He studied in Havana, Barcelona, and Madrid. Having fled to Paris because of the Spanish Civil War, he was introduced by Picasso to the Surrealist group. He soon became acquainted with André Breton, Max Ernst, and Brauner.

In 1941 Lam returned to Cuba with Breton, Masson, and Levi-Strauss, and this reintroduction to his native land gave his imagination a decisive new drive. His confrontation with the dramatic landscape of Haiti in 1947 was also important for him. He then went back to Europe to make his home, but continued to make frequent trips back and forth.

From the publication of *First Papers of Surrealism* in New York in 1942, Lam took an active part in all the major shows of the Surrealist group and in discussions of Surrealist theory, to which he contributed his own animism. His was the voice of tropical myth-making and Afro-Cuban totemism.

RENÉ MAGRITTE

Born on November 28, 1898, in Lessines, Belgium. He studied at the Academy of Fine Arts in Brussels and, in 1920, met E. L. T. Mesens. In order to make a living, Magritte worked in a wallpaper factory, where he met Victor Servrauczk. In his own work his experiments were tending toward the late Cubist style until, in 1923, he discovered the metaphysical paintings of de Chirico.

With Marcel Lecomte, Camille Goemaus, Paul Nougé, and Mesens, he started a movement that was close to Surrealism in Belgium through the publication of magazines: *Œ sophage, Marie,* and *Correspondence.* In 1926 this group entered into direct contact with the Paris Bretonists. Between 1927 and 1930 Magritte lived in France near Paris and played an active role in the undertakings of the Surrealists. He then returned to Brussels, where the Belgian adherents to Surrealism had become more numerous and active.

Between 1951 and 1953, Magritte decorated the Casino at Knokke. He died in Brussels in 1967.

ALBERTO MARTINI

Born in Oderzo near Treviso, Italy, November 24, 1876. He began work as an illustrator in 1895. Between 1900 and 1920 his ''black humor,'' with its first traces of Symbolist feeling, expressed itself in decidedly pre-Surrealist works (the illustrations

MAGRITTE *Illumination,* 1934, Turin, private collection

of Edgar Allan Poe's work in 1906, and the lithographs of two series, *Danse Macabre* and *Les Mystères*). In 1928 Martini went to Paris, where he stayed until the beginning of World War II. Martini was extremely productive as a painter from the end of the 1920s until his death in Milan in 1954.

ANDRÉ MASSON

Born in Balaguy, France, January 4, 1896. Through Max Jacob he met Kahnweiler in 1922 and, in the following year, Artaud, Leiris, Limbour, and Miró. Breton bought his painting *The Four Ele-*

ments. In 1924 Masson became a member of the Surrealist group and took part in all its activities. He broke with the group in 1929, yet contributed to the Surrealist shows in London in 1936, in New York in 1937, and in Paris in 1938. From 1941 to 1945 he lived in the United States, part of the time in New Preston, Connecticut. During his stay he strongly influenced the new North American painting.

Masson has been particularly productive as an etcher. He has also made numerous contributions to theoretical literature. He now lives in Tholonet, near Aix-en-Provence.

MATTA

Born in Santiago, Chile, November 11, 1911. After he had completed studies in architecture, he went to Europe and worked for Le Corbusier from 1935 to 1937. Garcia Lorca introduced him to Dali, and, in 1937, when he had been drawing for about a year, he met André Breton. In 1938 he began to paint. His canvases, which he called "psychological morphology," almost immediately achieved exceptional intensity and a highly personal quality that fascinated Breton, who recognized in Matta's works a most definite appearance of "absolute automatism."

MARTINI *Visions of the Dead Lover,* 1905, Milan, Renato Morganti Collection

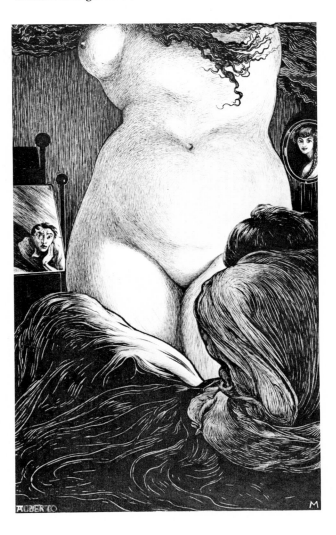

In 1939 Matta went to the United States, where his first one-man shows were held. In 1948 he was read out of the Surrealist group. He returned to

MASSON *Armor,* 1925

Europe, lived in Rome between 1950 and 1954, and then settled in Paris. In 1959 he officially reentered Surrealist circles. As well as other meanings, he attributes political significance to his paintings, defining them as anti-imperialist and anti-colonial.

MIKULAS MEDET

Born in Prague in 1926 and studied at the State School of Graphics. He went on to the High School of Art and to the Academy of Fine Arts, where he was a student of Muzika and of Tichy. After his Surrealist experiments, which began in the last years of the 1940s and lasted throughout the 1950s, he contributed as a leader to the informal Czech group of Surrealists, bringing to the group his own imagery of magical tension.

JOAN MIRÓ

Born in Barcelona, April 20, 1893, the son of a goldsmith and cabinetmaker. He began to paint in 1912, feeling drawn toward Fauvism. In 1918 he devoted himself to highly analytic painting. A year later he went to Paris and met Picasso, Reverdy, and finally Tzara. Through them he became friends with Masson, Leiris, and Prévert, and in the summer of 1923 he painted, in Montroig, canvases that were turning points in his career as a Surrealist painter. The following year he met Breton, Eluard, and Aragon, and from then on took part in the activity of the movement.

When the Nazis occupied France, he returned to Spain, first to Montroig, then to Palma de Majorca, and finally to Barcelona. His work, extremely relevant from the graphic point of view, included ceramics—in collaboration with Artigas—which he produced in thematically and formally defined cycles. In the 1940s his *Constellations* were famous, and in the succeeding decade he interpreted the extreme need for immediacy by using a "spotting" technique relating to other informal experiments. Miró now lives between Palma de Majorca and Barcelona.

FRANTISEK MUZIKA

Born in Prague, June 26, 1900. He studied there at the Academy of Fine Arts, and in 1920, while still a student, he became a member of the avant-garde group called Devetsil. He showed at the exhibition *Poésie 1923* in Prague. In the period between 1920 and 1925, his paintings resembled the primitivistic, magic realism that resolved itself between 1926 and 1931 in a particularly lyric form of the late Cubist tradition. His adventures in imaginative exploration began in the early 1930s. He was always strongly interested in stage design, and he is a student of handwriting, a subject on which he has written a detailed treatise.

Frantisek Muzika now lives in Prague.

RICHARD ŒLZE

Born in Magdeburg, Germany, June 29, 1900. He

Miró *Drawing and Collage*, 1933 (70 x 100 cm) Rome, Claudio Cavazza Collection

studied at the Bauhaus in Weimar and followed it to Dessau. In 1933, in Paris, he came into contact with Breton, Dali, Eluard, and Max Ernst, and the birth of his Surrealist painting dates from the following year. He developed his own version of *frottage*, "a personal solution of automatism which opens a universe turned topsy-turvy by furious winds and crossed by flying phantoms" (Pierre).

Œlze's work as a painter was inevitably inter-

rupted during the Nazi period and war years between 1936 and 1946. But after the Nazi collapse, he picked up the threads of his own experiments with the greatest coherence and consistency. He now lives near Hameln, Germany.

WOLGANG PAALEN

Born in Vienna in 1905. He studied painting in Italy, Berlin, Paris, and Munich. Before joining the

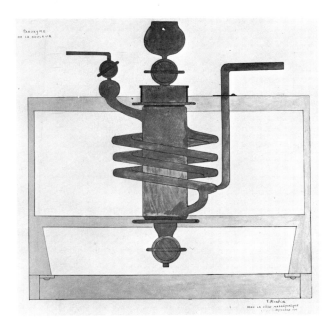

Picabia *Paroxyme* (sic) *de la Douleur*, 1915, Paris, Simone Collinet Collection

Surrealists in 1936, he played an active role in the Abstraction-Creation group. He contributed to the invention of figurative techniques among the Surrealists with his *frottage*, obtaining exceptional results from its use.

In 1939 he went to Mexico, where he stayed until 1951, and where, in 1940, he organized, together with the Peruvian Surrealist poet Cesar Moro, the International Exposition of Surrealism. In 1942 he founded the magazine *Dyn*, and he withdrew somewhat from the Surrealist movement for a few years. At that time his painting was enriched by a variety of experiences, among the foremost of which was his own informal type of "abstract lyricism."

He went back to Paris in 1952, having drawn nearer the Surrealists during the previous two years, and once more he took part in the group's activities.

In 1954 he returned to Mexico, where he died in 1959.

FRANCIS PICABIA

Born in Paris, January 22, 1879, of a Cuban father and a French mother. After periods of both Impressionist work, related to Pissarro, and Post-Impressionist work, Picabia achieved his own version of Cubism about 1910. In 1915 he went with Duchamp and Man Ray to New York, where they enlivened its Dadaist movement. In Barcelona, in 1917, he founded the Dadaist review *391,* and at this time he came into close contact with Tzara, whom he later welcomed to Paris.

Picabia continued his trailblazing activities with the magazines *Cannibale* and *La Pomme de Pin.* His poetic production was as rich as his painting and experimentation. Many drawings, too, appeared in *Littérature* and other Surrealist reviews. After 1925 he lived on the Côte d'Azur, but returned to Paris in 1945. He died there in 1953. The international nomadic life at its highest level was compatible with his personality as an artist and as a man.

MAN RAY

Born in Philadelphia in 1890. He grew up in New York, attended school there, and later participated in the Dadaist activities of Duchamp and Picabia. In 1921 he moved to Paris, where he invented his "rayograms." He was always broadly interested in photography and cinema and in the production of objects, though all this did not distract him from his painting. His first films were *Emak Bakia* in 1926, *Etoile de mer* in 1928, and *Mystère au Château de Dés* in 1929.

In 1940 he returned to the United States but went back to Paris again in 1949, where he continues to live and work. He published *Self-Portrait* in 1953.

RAY *Rayogramme,* 1921

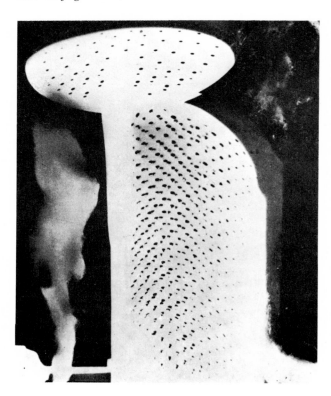

ALBERTO SAVINIO

Born in Athens, August 25, 1891, the younger brother of Giorgio de Chirico. He began his career in music, studying in Munich. He was also ex-

tremely interested in literature. In 1910, in Paris, while continuing to work predominantly in music, he started to write *(Les Chants de la Mi-Mort, 1914).* He became a friend of Apollinaire and contributed to *291,* which was published in New York. Returning to Italy in 1915, he joined de Chirico and Carrà in Ferrara, and he kept in close touch with Tzara through his collaboration with *Dada.* In 1918 he collected in a single issue of *Hermafrodito* the pieces he had written in previous years, some of which had already been published. He went back to Paris in 1925 and began to dedicate himself unremittingly to painting.

Savinio returned to Italy in 1934, where his work was again largely literary and, from 1946 on, once more musical. He died in Rome in 1952.

JOSEPH SIMA

Born in Jaroma, a small city in Bohemia, Czechoslovakia, March 19, 1891. He was the son of an architect and professor of painting at the School of Arts and Trades. He studied at the Academy of Fine Arts in Prague and was a pupil of the great Czech Symbolist painter Jan Preisler, whose works profoundly influenced Sima's formative years. After World War I, he moved to France, a tradition among major Czech contemporary artists such as Mucha, Kupka, and Guttfreund. He settled in Paris in 1921, yet remained closely attached to the Czech avant-garde, directed at this time by Karel Teige.

In 1924, on Lake Lugano, he had a revelation or vision, as he had had a few years earlier in the south of France. "In that briefest instant of silent flashes of lightning that ran between clouds laden with electricity, the stripped nakedness of a dead tree appeared and was as suddenly eclipsed. It was truly a naked body. The light, grown denser, was creating the world."

In 1926 Sima met Breton, with whom, however, he formed no close friendship as he had with Eluard, Ernst, Soupault, Giacometti, and Leiris. In 1929 he founded—together with Roger Gilbert, Le Comte, René Daumal, Maurice Henry, Roger Vaillant, Artur Harfaux, and André Roland de Renéville—a group known as the Grand Ten, whose mystical orientation caused its break with the Bretonists.

During the 1930s Sima's painting was rich with the qualities of abstract lyricism; his experiments have followed this direction up to this day. Sima is currently living in Paris.

JINDRICH STYRSKY

Born in Cermna, near Kysperk, Czechoslovakia, August 11, 1899. In 1919, he painted his first pictures in the Cubist vein, and in 1923 he became, along with Toyen (Maria Germinova), who had emerged the previous year, a member of the Devetsil group (*see* Muzika). It was at this time that he painted his cycle of "pictorial poems"—between Dadaism and Surrealism. In 1925 he went to Paris with Toyen and they stayed there four years. That period saw the development of "Artificialism," whose manifesto of 1927 was published in the magazine *Red* (No. 1). Between 1929 and 1931 they passed from Artificialism to Surrealism, and Styrsky exhibited at the Poésie 1932 show in Prague. In 1934 he and Toyen were among the founders of the Czech Surrealist group, whose first show in the following year was the occasion of Breton and Eluard's visit to Prague.

Styrsky's work as an artist was intense and included collage, photomontage, and Surrealist photography, as well as painting. In 1939 Nazi censorship forbade Styrsky and Toyen any public activity, but they published drawings, collages, and photographs in the clandestine edition of *Le Serv.* In 1940 Styrsky finished his *Book of Dreams,* which contained drawings, collages, paintings, and even the written record of his dreams from 1925 to 1940.

He died of a heart attack in Prague in 1942.

MAX WALTER SVANBERG

Born in Malmö, Sweden, February 20, 1912. His first Surrealist drawings appeared between 1943 and 1944, by which time he was already attracted to heroic subjects.

Between 1946 and 1948 he was a member of *The Minotaure* group, and in 1950 he founded the Imago movement.

In 1953 he established contact with Breton, who introduced Svanberg's one-man show in Paris in 1955 at the Etoile Scellée. Svanberg now lives in Malmö.

Styrsky *Temporale,* 1927

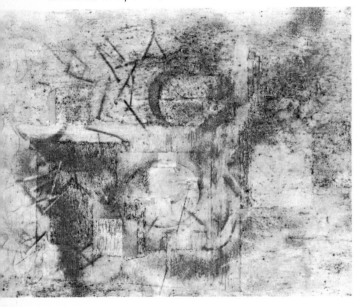

Toyen *Two Drawings from the Series "Le Tir,"* 1939–40, Paris, collection of the artist

his painting was already revealing a personal style.

In 1939 he left with Kay Sage for New York, and in 1942 he settled in Woodbury, Connecticut, and became a United States citizen. He died there in 1955.

TOYEN

Born in Prague, September 21, 1902. By the middle 1920s her painting had moved from a brief, late-Cubist style to one that expressed exotic and popular reveries. She was a member of the Devetsil group in whose ambience she developed "poetism," founded on the refusal of a standard aesthetics, the identity of poetry and painting, and the primacy of the unconscious. A type of lyric abstraction was born from it, which she, along with her companion Styrsky, formulated in a manifesto on Artificialism in 1927. From the 1930s on, her driving, imaginative experiments took many varied forms and were related to both the metaphysical and the Surrealist traditions.

Toyen came into contact with Breton at the time of his and Eluard's visit to Prague in 1935. During World War II she completed two graphic series that were true acts of revolt: *Marksmanship,* in 1940, and *Hide, War,* in 1944. In 1947 she went back to Paris, taking part in all the activities of the Surrealist group to which she still belongs.

YVES TANGUY

Born in Paris, January 5, 1900, of Breton parents. His father was a navy officer, a career toward which Tanguy himself was first drawn. In 1922 he met Jacques Prévert, and the following year he discovered in the Paul Guillaume Gallery a painting by de Chirico that greatly influenced him. He began to teach himself to paint, and in 1925 he subscribed to Surrealism. The following year

List of Illustrations

Translated by Frances H. Keene

Permission by A.D.A.G.P. by French Reproduction Rights 1970, for the works of Hans Arp, Hans Bellmer, Marcel Duchamp, René Magritte, André Masson, Joan Miro, Francis Picabia, Man Ray

Permission by S.P.A.D.E.M. by French Reproduction Rights 1970, for the works of Max Ernst, Paul Klee, Pablo Picasso